American Moments

ABDO
& Daughters

THE MONTGOMERY BUS BOYCOTT

By Alan Pierce

"EASE THAT SQUEEZE"
RIDE THE BUS

VISIT US AT
WWW.ABDOPUB.COM

Edited by: Melanie A. Howard
Interior Production and Design: Terry Dunham Incorporated
Cover Design: Mighty Media
Photos: AP/Wide World, Corbis, Library of Congress, North Wind Pictures

Library of Congress Cataloging-in-Publication Data

Pierce, Alan, 1966-
   The Montgomery bus boycott / Alan Pierce.
      p. cm. -- (American moments)
   Includes index.
   ISBN 1-59197-935-8
   1. African Americans--Civil rights--Alabama--Montgomery--History--20th century--Juvenile literature. 2. Civil rights movements--Alabama--Montgomery--History--20th century--Juvenile literature. 3. Segregation in transportation--Alabama--Montgomery--Juvenile literature. 4. African American civil rights workers--Alabama--Montgomery--History--20th century--Juvenile literature. 5. Montgomery (Ala.)--Race relations--Juvenile literature. I. Title. II. Series.

F334.M79N457 2005
323.1196'073076147--dc22
                                                           2004062377

CONTENTS

ROSA PARKS

Rosa Parks was tired after a busy day at work. She was a seamstress at a department store in downtown Montgomery, Alabama. On December 1, 1955, customers had kept her busy fitting their clothes for the Christmas season.

After her long day, Parks boarded a bus to go home. At this time, seating on Montgomery buses was separated by race. The first ten seats were reserved for white passengers. African-American passengers occupied the rear ten seats. Passengers in the middle seats were separated so that black and white riders did not sit in the same row. In addition, blacks had to give up their seats to whites if no other seats were available.

Parks was an African-American woman, so she rode in a seat reserved for black passengers. At one stop, a white man boarded the bus. All the seats were occupied. Bus driver J.F. Blake told Parks and three other African-American riders to give up their seats.

Three of the African-American passengers stood up. Parks refused. She was tired from working hard. But she was even more tired of being bullied because of her race. Blake called the police, who arrested Parks and took her to jail.

Rosa Parks is fingerprinted after being arrested for not giving up her bus seat.

News of Parks's arrest spread among African Americans in the city. Leaders in Montgomery's African-American community organized a boycott of the buses. They demanded better treatment of African-American riders. Parks's single act of defiance had inspired a protest that included thousands of African Americans. The Montgomery bus boycott had begun.

JIM CROW

The mistreatment of African Americans did not begin on buses in Montgomery. The abuse of blacks had a long history in the United States. In the seventeenth century, laborers were needed to plant and harvest tobacco in the British colony of Virginia. To meet this demand for labor, Europeans shipped captive Africans to North America. These Africans worked as slaves on tobacco, rice, and indigo plantations.

Slaves occupied a low place in society. They were considered property and served their masters for life. Also, the children of slave mothers inherited their status as slaves. In this way, families remained slaves from generation to generation.

Slavery continued even after the 13 American colonies had won their independence from Britain in 1783. Slavery mainly existed in the southern part of the country. In the late eighteenth and early nineteenth centuries, cotton became a more profitable crop. Large numbers of slaves were needed to produce this crop in Southern states.

Slaves arrive in the colony of Virginia.

Slaves work on a cotton plantation.

Many people in the North opposed slavery for moral reasons. They believed it was wrong for one person to own another person. Gradually, the Northern states banned slavery. By the early nineteenth century, slavery had been abolished in the North.

The nation's bitter divide over slavery helped lead to the Civil War. In 1860, Abraham Lincoln was elected president of the United States. He was a well-known opponent of slavery. His election prompted 11 Southern states to secede from the nation. This caused the Civil War to break out between the Northern and Southern states in 1861.

After four years of brutal fighting, the North's armies vanquished the South's forces. Many Northern leaders believed a constitutional amendment was needed to end slavery. In 1865, the Thirteenth

Amendment was passed. This made slavery illegal in the United States. In 1868, the Fourteenth Amendment was ratified. This amendment was intended to guarantee state and U.S. citizenship to African Americans.

The Fourteenth Amendment also included an important guarantee known as equal protection. Equal protection means the government is required to treat people in a similar way who are in similar situations. This guarantee was supposed to guard African Americans against discrimination.

In 1870, Congress and the states added another constitutional protection for African Americans. On March 30, the Fifteenth Amendment was ratified. This amendment was intended to protect the voting rights of American-American men.

Unfortunately, these constitutional amendments did little to help African Americans. Whites in the South found ways to trample on African-American rights. Violent organizations such as the Ku Klux Klan formed. Members of the Klan wore white sheets to disguise their identity from U.S. soldiers stationed in the South. The Klan committed acts of violence to terrify African Americans. One goal of the Klan was to prevent African Americans from voting.

White Southerners used other means to deny African Americans the right to vote. Southern states established a poll tax. Those who wished to vote had to pay the tax before they voted. The tax discouraged many African Americans from voting because they could not afford it.

Many Southern states also set up literacy tests to keep African Americans from voting. The tests often required people to interpret difficult documents such as part of the state constitution.

A voting official then determined whether the document had been interpreted correctly.

In the South, a system known as segregation separated blacks and whites in public places. This practice was commonly called Jim Crow. The name *Jim Crow* arose from a musical performance staged by a white minstrel named Thomas Dartmouth Rice. He performed this routine in the late 1820s and 1830s. No one is certain why segregation was later referred to as Jim Crow.

Segregation grew more prevalent in the South in the 1890s. Jim Crow laws separated blacks and whites in parks, hospitals, restaurants,

Ku Klux Klan members hold an African-American man captive.

and even cemeteries. Black and white children also attended separate schools. But the facilities for white students were almost always superior to the facilities for black students.

Public transportation was also segregated. In Louisiana, a group of African Americans decided to fight against segregation on railroad cars. In June 1892, a man of African-American descent named Homer Plessy attempted to board a railroad car reserved for white passengers. He was arrested for breaking the state's segregation law. Judge John H. Ferguson found Plessy guilty, but Plessy filed a lawsuit against the judge.

The case of *Plessy v. Ferguson* went to the U.S. Supreme Court in 1896. The Court upheld Louisiana's segregation law by developing the "separate but equal" doctrine. This doctrine held that segregated facilities were legal as long as they were equal. The Supreme Court's decision had a significant impact on the nation. The Court had given legal protection to racial segregation.

Whites denied political and legal rights to African Americans. Sometimes white mobs murdered African Americans who were thought to have committed crimes. In other cases, whites killed African Americans who attempted to vote or who were considered disrespectful to whites.

In 1909, African Americans and whites concerned about this violence met in New York City, New York. They formed an organization that soon became known as the National Association for the Advancement of Colored People (NAACP). This organization worked for stronger laws to punish those who committed violence against African Americans.

The NAACP also fought in the courtroom for the rights of African Americans. Lawyers for the NAACP won victories against voting discrimination. They also won court cases to enroll African Americans in law schools. In 1940, the NAACP Legal Defense and Educational Fund (LDF) was established. This organization continued the legal fight for African Americans. Thurgood Marshall, who had been an NAACP lawyer, headed the LDF.

Thurgood Marshall helped Ada Lois Sipuel gain admission to the previously all-white University of Oklahoma School of Law in 1948. J.E. Fellows reads Sipuel's college record while seated next to her. Standing from the left are attorney D.H. Williams, Marshall, and Oklahoma state representative Amos Hall.

SHAME OF SEGREGATION

In Montgomery, segregation was a shameful experience for African-American bus riders. No African Americans drove buses in Montgomery. White bus drivers possessed all the authority on the buses. Drivers were frequently rude to African-American passengers. After African Americans paid their bus fare, they had to reenter the bus in the back. Sometimes bus drivers drove off while African Americans were walking to board the back of the bus.

Some African Americans refused to accept this harassment. Women were especially active. Mary Burks was committed to improving the lives of African Americans. She was an English professor at Alabama State College in Montgomery. In 1946, Burks formed the Women's Political Council.

At first, the organization encouraged African Americans to register to vote. But another professor at the college experienced a disturbing incident on a Montgomery bus. In 1949, Jo Ann Robinson was riding on a bus with only a couple of other passengers. The driver yelled at her to give up her seat. She thought the driver might strike her.

Like Burks, Robinson was also a member of the Women's Political Council. After Robinson's upsetting encounter, the organization focused on improving conditions for African Americans on the buses.

A Montgomery, Alabama, city bus

The Women's Political Council favored the seating arrangement used on buses in Mobile, Alabama. Seating was still segregated in Mobile, but no riders had to give up their seats. In the fall of 1952, the organization asked city officials to adopt Mobile's seating policy. But the seating arrangement in Montgomery remained the same.

Montgomery was not the only Southern city where segregated buses caused tensions. African Americans and whites also disagreed about enforcement of segregation in Baton Rouge, Louisiana. The dispute involved a city ordinance that took effect in March 1953. The ordinance did not forbid segregation on buses. But it did allow seating to take place on a first-come, first-serve basis. Bus drivers ignored the ordinance, which upset African Americans.

Louisiana's attorney general announced that the ordinance was illegal. African-American leaders planned a bus boycott. They also organized a car pool to give boycotters rides. Among the leaders were the Reverend Theodore J. Jemison and Raymond Scott, a tailor. They announced the bus boycott and the availability of the car pool on the radio.

The boycott lasted for about a week. By then, the Baton Rouge city council agreed to a compromise. The first two seats on buses were reserved for whites. The last two seats were reserved for African Americans. Riders of any race were allowed to sit anywhere else on the bus.

Meanwhile, segregation in education came under attack. Lawyers for the NAACP Legal Defense Fund filed lawsuits claiming that segregated public schools were unconstitutional. Eventually, the U.S. Supreme Court decided to review cases from Delaware, Kansas, South Carolina, and Virginia. These cases were combined under the name of *Brown v. Board of Education of Topeka*.

On May 17, 1954, U.S. Supreme Court justice Earl Warren announced the Court's decision. He declared that segregation had no place in public schools. The Court had rejected the "separate but equal" doctrine of the *Plessy* case.

The Supreme Court's decision did not suddenly end segregation. In fact, the Alabama State Board of Education decided to maintain segregation in schools for another year. The Alabama legislature also rejected the Supreme Court's ruling. Throughout the South, whites vowed to fight integration.

Defense attorneys E.C. Hayes (left), Thurgood Marshall (center), and James Madison Nabrit Jr. congratulate each other after the Brown v. Board of Education *victory.*

THE BOYCOTT BEGINS

African Americans in Montgomery considered their own strategies for battling segregation. E.D. Nixon wished to challenge segregation on the city's buses. Nixon was one of Montgomery's best-known African-American leaders. He had served as president of the Alabama chapter of the NAACP. In addition, he worked as a porter on railroad sleeping cars. He led the local labor union of sleeping car porters.

In order to fight segregation on the buses, Nixon wanted to organize a protest or file a lawsuit. He waited for an incident that would rally African Americans. On March 2, 1955, an African-American teenager named Claudette Colvin refused to give up her seat to white passengers. Colvin fought police when they arrived, and officers took her away in handcuffs.

The police's treatment of Colvin angered African Americans. Nixon talked to Colvin and her family. Based on these discussions, Nixon did not think Colvin could bear being the focus of a protest.

Several months later, another African-American teenager challenged segregated seating. On October 21, Mary Louise Smith was arrested for not giving up her seat to a white passenger. Smith's arrest caused more outrage among African Americans. But she pleaded guilty, and anger over the arrest faded.

E.D. Nixon stands next to Rosa Parks as she speaks to a reporter.

Then on December 1, Rosa Parks refused to give up her bus seat. She was arrested and taken to jail. Nixon learned of Parks's arrest from a woman who had been on the bus. He contacted a white lawyer named Clifford Durr. Durr gained information about the charges against Parks and the amount of her bail. Nixon went to the jail where he paid Parks's $100 bail. She was released from custody.

News of Parks's arrest angered African Americans in Montgomery. She served as secretary of the Montgomery chapter of the NAACP and had a friendly personality. Her role with the NAACP and her character made her a respected member of the African-American community.

African-American leaders responded quickly. Fred D. Gray was one of the few African-American lawyers in Montgomery. He called Robinson, who had become president of the Women's Political Council. She contacted Nixon. They agreed to call for a bus boycott to protest Parks's arrest.

Robinson typed an announcement urging people to stay off the buses on Monday, December 5. Copies of the message were distributed throughout the African-American areas of the city.

Nixon also contacted African-American ministers to gain their support for the boycott. One person he called was a minister named Martin Luther King Jr. King served as pastor at Dexter Avenue Baptist Church. He had lived in northern states where he attended seminary and worked on an advanced degree in theology. But King was also familiar with segregation and the struggles of African Americans in the South. He had grown up in Atlanta, Georgia. In that city, King's father, the Reverend Martin Luther King Sr., served as a minister.

On December 2, several African-American ministers and other leaders met at Dexter Avenue Baptist Church. During this meeting, they agreed to support the protest. They also realized that transportation would be a problem for the boycotters. Fortunately, there were several taxi companies operated by African Americans in Montgomery. Some people at the meeting agreed to see if these companies would transport people during the boycott.

The boycott on Monday, December 5 was a success. Almost no African Americans rode the buses that day. All the taxi companies owned by African Americans agreed to provide rides. But African

Martin Luther King Jr.

Americans found other ways to travel. Many walked. A few even rode mules or used horse-drawn carriages.

That same morning, Parks appeared in court for her trial. Fred D. Gray, who was Parks's friend, represented her in court. The trial attracted a lot of interest. The segregated courtroom was filled with African Americans and whites. Hundreds of African Americans also gathered outside the courthouse to show support for Parks.

Judge John Scott found Parks guilty of breaking a state segregation law. She was fined $10 and ordered to pay $4 in court costs. Gray, however, planned to appeal Parks's case. He wanted to use the case to challenge segregation laws in higher courts.

After Parks's trial, Nixon and other African-American leaders saw the need for an organization to lead the protest. They met at Mount Zion African Methodist Episcopal Zion Church. One of the first orders of business was to elect officers.

Rufus Lewis, a local businessman, nominated King for president. The group approved the nomination, much to King's surprise. He was 26 years old and a newcomer to Montgomery. However, King's short time in Montgomery helped his nomination. He had not lived in Montgomery long enough to make enemies.

Those who attended the meeting considered names for the organization. A few names were suggested, but they were rejected. Finally, the Reverend Ralph Abernathy suggested Montgomery Improvement Association (MIA). This became the group's name.

That night there was a public meeting at Holt Street Baptist Church. Thousands of African Americans celebrated the widespread participation in the boycott. Rosa Parks received a standing ovation. King delivered a powerful speech. He described Parks's arrest and recounted the history of abuse that African Americans had suffered on the buses. But King also encouraged boycotters to refrain from violence.

Abernathy read a resolution of demands sought by African-American riders. These demands included polite treatment by bus drivers, and hiring African American drivers for routes used mainly by African-American riders. The resolution also called for seating on a first-come, first-serve basis. Black riders would be seated from

Ralph Abernathy

back to front while white riders would be seated from front to back.

The resolution also supported continuation of the boycott until these demands were met. Thousands of people cheered the resolution, which ensured that the boycott would continue.

CAR POOL

Leaders of the MIA expected to reach an agreement quickly with city and bus officials. King and other MIA members believed their demands were reasonable. They did not seek to end segregation on buses. Instead, MIA members wanted better treatment for African Americans.

On December 8, members of the MIA met with city officials and representatives from the Montgomery City Lines bus company. However, no progress was made throughout the month. It became clear to many MIA members that city officials did not want to compromise.

Gray supported a different approach. He wanted to file a lawsuit that challenged the constitutionality of segregated seating. Moreover, he wished to file the lawsuit in federal district court. Gray favored this approach because a lawsuit in federal court would go faster to the U.S. Supreme Court than a lawsuit filed in state district court. But some MIA members still held out hope that an agreement could be reached.

Meanwhile, the MIA was presented with the challenge of transporting the boycotters. City officials had hinted that the use of the taxis in the boycott was illegal. About 17,500 African Americans had ridden buses twice a day. They needed a way to get to and from work. The MIA set up a transportation committee to address this problem.

Fred D. Gray

King was aware of the bus boycott in Baton Rouge. He called Jemison, who was a friend of King's family. Jemison told King about the car pool they had organized during the boycott. King then informed the transportation committee about the operation of the car pool in Baton Rouge.

The MIA announced the need for volunteer drivers and cars to start a car pool in Montgomery. The response was astonishing. At first, about 150 people volunteered to drive. Eventually, the number of volunteers climbed to about 300. In addition to providing rides, the MIA also set up dispatch and pick up centers. By December 13, the MIA had established a well-run car pool.

Operating the car pool and the MIA, however, cost money. About $5,000 was needed every month to pay expenses. But the Montgomery bus boycott was also receiving news coverage from around the world. This publicity helped the boycott. People became aware of the struggle in Montgomery and donated money. These donations allowed the MIA to purchase more than 15 new station wagons for the car pool.

City leaders responded to the boycott with a tougher approach. Mayor W.A. Gayle asked white employers not to drive black employees to work. Police officers began to stop and harass car pool drivers. African Americans waiting for car pool rides were also harassed. Police warned boycotters about laws against hitchhiking. These tactics had some effect. A few drivers dropped out of the car pool.

On January 26, 1956, King became the target of this harassment. In downtown Montgomery, he picked up three people who lived on the way to his home. As he left the parking lot, police officers on

In the middle of the day, a Montgomery bus is empty
due to the continuing success of the boycott.

motorcycles followed King's car. When King dropped off some of his passengers, police arrested King for speeding. They accused King of driving 30 mph (48 km/h) in a 25 mph (40 km/h) zone. Officers then took King to the Montgomery city jail.

African Americans in Montgomery soon learned of King's arrest. Abernathy managed to obtain enough money to pay cash for King's bail. King was released from jail the same day he was arrested. But King still faced a trial for the speeding charge.

KING'S DEVOTION TO PEACE

Jail was only one example of the harassment that King faced. Every day he received threatening letters and telephone calls at his home. King had even learned that some people were plotting to kill him.

On the night of January 30, 1956, King's wife, Coretta, and their baby daughter, Yolanda, were at home. A member of King's church, Mary Lucy Williams, stayed with Coretta while Martin Luther King Jr. attended a meeting. The two women heard something land on the porch. They moved to the back of the house. A bomb exploded, shattering windows in the home. But the two women and the baby were unharmed.

King learned of the explosion and quickly returned home. He made sure that Coretta and Yolanda were safe. Then he spoke to the crowd of African Americans who had gathered outside his home. They were angry about the attack, and many of them were armed.

King urged the crowd to remain calm. He also urged the crowd to listen to Montgomery police commissioner Clyde Sellers. Sellers announced a reward for information about whomever had committed the bombing. Afterward, the crowd broke up without any violent acts.

The attack on King's home and the harassment of car pool drivers changed the minds of the boycott's leaders. They decided to support

NONVIOLENCE

Martin Luther King Jr. believed in a method of protest known as "nonviolent resistance." This strategy seeks to avoid violent conflicts. Those who engage in nonviolent resistance attempt to sway their oppressors. The goal of this method is to make oppressors realize they are wrong to commit injustice.

King favored nonviolent resistance because it fit with his Christian values. However, King learned about this method from his study of Mohandas Karamchand

Mohandas Karamchand Gandhi

Gandhi. For several decades in the twentieth century, Gandhi had helped lead the effort to free India from British rule. He used nonviolent means to resist the British. For example, he organized an Indian boycott of British manufacturers, schools, and courts. India achieved independence in 1947. Gandhi did not live to see an independent India for very long. He was killed on January 30, 1948.

Gray's idea for a federal lawsuit. On February 1, Gray filed the federal lawsuit in the U.S. District Court in Montgomery. The lawsuit took aim at segregation laws in the city of Montgomery and the state of Alabama. Gray wanted to use the lawsuit to find these laws unconstitutional.

The lawsuit was called *Browder v. Gayle*. Browder was the last name of Amelia Browder, the first plaintiff in the case. She was one of five plaintiffs listed in the lawsuit. The others were Susie McDonald, Jeanetta Reese, Colvin, and Smith. Reese soon withdrew her name from the case.

Gray decided not to include Parks in the case. He did not want her criminal case to become an issue in the lawsuit. Gray wanted to focus strictly on the constitutionality of Montgomery's and Alabama's segregation laws.

To prepare for the case, Gray also consulted with LDF attorneys Thurgood Marshall and Robert Carter. Marshall, Carter, and Charles Langford joined Gray as attorneys in *Browder v. Gayle*.

Mayor Gayle was the first defendant listed in the case. But other Montgomery city officials were named as well. Commissioners Sellers and Frank Parks were listed in the lawsuit. Police chief Goodwin J. Ruppenthal was also named in the suit. The lawsuit also named Montgomery City Lines bus company and two bus drivers as defendants. Meanwhile, violence continued to occur. On February 1, someone threw a stick of dynamite in Nixon's yard. Fortunately, no one was hurt in the attack.

White leaders tried another tactic to weaken the boycott. They cited an Alabama law that prohibited boycotts in certain cases. In

Ralph Abernathy (center) *watches as King* (right) *is booked at the Montgomery police station for breaking a boycott law.*

February, members of a grand jury found the boycott illegal. Furthermore, the jury found that more than 100 people should be charged with breaking this law.

King was among those the jury had accused. King's father feared for his son's safety. King Sr. urged his son to leave Montgomery. Martin Luther King Jr. believed he would look like a coward if he left the city. He decided to turn himself in to authorities at the jail. There, a member of King's church paid his bail and King was allowed to leave.

King speaks to reporters before his trial.

The trial began on March 19. King had plenty of public support. Hundreds of African Americans appeared at the courthouse where the trial took place. Ministers from other areas of the country also attended the trial. King's trial also received global media coverage. Reporters from Europe, Asia, and the United States wrote about the trial.

During the trial, several African Americans testified about the cruelties they had suffered on Montgomery's buses. One woman shared a story about her husband. He had paid his fare but saw there was no room in the back of the bus. He offered to walk if the bus driver returned the 10¢ fare. The driver refused and an argument broke out. Police arrived and ended up shooting the man, who later died from the wound.

The trial ended on March 22. Judge Eugene Carter found King guilty of breaking the anti-boycott law. The judge sentenced King to 386 days of hard labor in jail. He also ordered King to pay a $500 fine. However, King did not go immediately to jail because his lawyers appealed the case. No other boycott leaders were tried until King's case was settled in appellate court.

Opposite page: *King and his wife, Coretta, walk out of the courthouse after King's trial.*

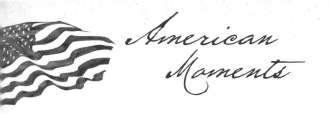

"WE ARE GLAD TO HAVE YOU"

The case of *Browder v. Gayle* was also proceeding that spring. On May 11, the hearing began before a three-judge panel in federal court. Robert Carter attacked the "separate but equal" doctrine. Attorneys for the city of Montgomery argued that ending segregation on buses would provoke violence.

After the hearing, judges Richard T. Rives, Frank M. Johnson, and Seybourn Lynne discussed the case. The Supreme Court's decision to end segregation in public schools influenced their talks. Johnson and Rives believed that the *Brown v. Board of Education* ruling meant that segregation was no longer legal. Lynne disagreed. He believed that the ruling applied only to segregation in public schools.

In early June, the three judges ruled 2–1 that bus segregation was unconstitutional. Rives and Johnson wrote that laws supporting bus segregation violated the Fourteenth Amendment. Lynne, however, asserted that the doctrine of "separate but equal" remained valid.

The federal judges' decision delighted African Americans in Montgomery. But the ruling failed to end segregation or the bus boycott. Mayor Gayle announced that the city would take the case to the U.S. Supreme Court. King said the boycott would continue until the Court had made its decision. The Supreme Court would not meet

FIGHTING SEGREGATION

The plaintiffs in the Brown v. Board of Education of Topeka case were not the first to fight segregation in public schools. The Legal Defense and Educational Fund (LDF) had been fighting segregation in schools for several years. However, members of LDF chose to challenge segregation in universities first.

Earl Warren

They began by demonstrating that African-American rights were being violated under the Plessy v. Ferguson "separate but equal" doctrine. In many areas, there were no equal university facilities available for African Americans. Case by case, the LDF chipped away at the "separate but equal" doctrine until it had been weakened enough to attack the doctrine itself. The LDF finally called "separate but equal" a violation of the Fourteenth Amendment in the Brown case.

The U.S. Supreme Court agreed. Justice Earl Warren declared that separating students "from others of a similar age and qualifications solely because of their race generates a feeling of inferiority … that may affect their hearts and minds in a way unlikely ever to be undone." A year after the ruling, the Supreme Court ordered that public schools be desegregated "with all deliberate speed."

until that fall. This meant the boycott would continue throughout the summer.

Montgomery city officials also decided to use the courts to halt the car pool, which had made the boycott a success. The city filed a lawsuit, seeking to stop the car pool. The MIA challenged the lawsuit but failed to prevent it. A hearing for the case was scheduled for November 13.

On that day, attorneys for the city and the MIA met before Judge Carter. Attorneys for the city argued that the car pool should be halted. They claimed the car pool was a private enterprise that required a license or franchise.

During the hearing, people in the courtroom learned from news reports that the Supreme Court had decided on the *Browder v. Gayle* case. Without a hearing, the Court had concluded that Montgomery's bus segregation law violated the Fourteenth Amendment. The Supreme Court's decision did not, however, prevent Judge Carter from ruling to halt the car pool.

November 13 was a day of both joy and distress for African Americans in Montgomery. The Supreme Court had ruled that segregation on Montgomery's buses was unconstitutional. But Judge Carter had stopped the car pool. Moreover, the MIA had decided to continue the boycott until the Supreme Court had issued an order for Montgomery to desegregate its buses. In the meantime, African Americans needed to find other transportation.

MIA leaders expected the Supreme Court's order to arrive within a few days. But the city of Montgomery requested a rehearing of the *Browder v. Gayle* case. This delayed the Court's order. The MIA

King rides a desegregated Montgomery city bus.
To his left is the Reverend Glenn Smiley.

scrambled to find ways for African Americans to get to work. It organized a system in which people in neighborhoods shared rides.

On December 20, the Supreme Court issued the final order that integrated Montgomery's buses. After 381 days, the boycott ended with a victory for African Americans. On December 21, King, Abernathy, and Nixon marked the event by boarding a bus. Reverend Glenn Smiley, a white Southerner, joined these men on the ride.

As they entered the bus, the driver asked King if he was the Reverend Martin Luther King Jr. King replied that he was. "We are glad to have you this morning," the bus driver said.

CIVIL RIGHTS ACT

Integration of Montgomery's buses did not go smoothly at first. MIA leaders and bus passengers were targeted for violence. On December 23, someone fired a shotgun at King's home. No one was injured. But people were hurt in later attacks. A few white men assaulted an African-American teenage girl after she exited a bus. On December 28, snipers fired at buses. Bullets struck the legs of an African-American woman named Rosa Jordan.

On January 10, 1957, a series of bombings blasted churches and homes in Montgomery. Bombs destroyed two African-American churches and damaged two others. A bomb also exploded at Abernathy's home. A sixth bomb caused major damage at the home of the Reverend Robert Graetz, a white leader in the MIA.

Several ministers and business leaders in the white community condemned the attacks. But the violence continued. On January 28, a bomb made of 12 sticks of dynamite was found on King's porch. King, who had been on the other side of town, returned home. Once again, a crowd formed around King's house. And once again, King urged people to be peaceful.

On January 30, authorities arrested seven men in connection with the bombings. They all belonged to the Ku Klux Klan. None of the

Part of the Bell Street Baptist Church was reduced to a pile of rubble during a wave of bombings on January 10, 1957.

men arrested for the bombings were found guilty. But violence subsided in Montgomery after the arrests, and people began to accept integrated buses.

The Montgomery bus boycott preceded other protests against segregation. Store lunch counters remained segregated in the South. On February 1, 1960, four African-American college students entered the Woolworth's store in Greensboro, North Carolina. Students Ezell Blair Jr., Franklin McCain, Joseph McNeil, and David Richmond sat at the counter where they were refused service. This type of protest is known as a sit-in.

More students joined the sit-in and the protest grew to include the Kress store. By July 1960, these two stores desegregated their

(From left to right) *Joseph McNeil, Franklin McCain, David Richmond, and Ezell Blair Jr. at a sit-in protest at Woolworth's in Greensboro, North Carolina*

lunch counters. Sit-ins spread to about 100 other Southern cities. Many stores in these cities also desegregated their counters.

The success of the sit-ins encouraged the Freedom Rides. This undertaking called for African-American and white activists to ride two buses from Washington DC to New Orleans, Louisiana. The purpose of the rides was to see whether a U.S. Supreme Court ruling was being obeyed. The Court had ruled that segregated bus stations and terminals that served interstate travelers were unconstitutional.

The Freedom Rides began on May 4, 1961. Many of the riders expected violence, and their fears were justified. A mob attacked one of the buses outside of Anniston, Alabama. A bomb thrown inside

Smoke billows out of the Freedom Riders' bus in Anniston, Alabama, after a bomb had set it on fire.

the bus exploded, forcing the riders to flee the bus. Riders on the second bus were attacked in Birmingham, Alabama. These riders flew to New Orleans.

Some activists were committed to finishing the ride. U.S. attorney general Robert F. Kennedy worked to make sure that Alabama and local officials protected the riders. However, violence still occurred. A mob used clubs and chains to beat riders at a Montgomery bus station. Members of the MIA saved the riders from more harm. After the Montgomery police failed to protect the riders, Kennedy acted. He ordered federal marshals to go to Montgomery to assure the riders' safety.

After the Freedom Rides, the federal government became more involved in the civil rights movement. Kennedy's brother was U.S. president John F. Kennedy. The two brothers became strong supporters of civil rights for African Americans. By 1963, President Kennedy supported a civil rights bill to fight racial discrimination. The bill, however, stalled in Congress.

On November 22, 1963, President Kennedy was assassinated in Dallas, Texas. Vice President Lyndon B. Johnson succeeded Kennedy as president. One of Johnson's first acts as president was to urge Congress to pass the civil rights bill.

With Johnson's support, the bill was approved by Congress on July 2, 1964. This legislation was known as the Civil Rights Act of 1964. It was stronger than the bill Kennedy had proposed. In fact, the act was regarded as the most important piece of civil rights legislation in 100 years.

The Civil Rights Act targeted segregation in public accommodations such as hotels, restaurants, and government buildings. In addition, the act gave the federal government more power to desegregate public schools. This authority was necessary because many school districts continued to resist integration.

The federal government had become committed to battling racial discrimination. The efforts of thousands of African Americans in Montgomery helped make this happen. African Americans organized the bus boycott, stood up for their rights, and gained the world's attention. And it all began when Rosa Parks refused to give up her bus seat.

President Lyndon B. Johnson shakes hands with Martin Luther King Jr. at the ceremony to sign the Civil Rights Act of 1964.

TIMELINE

1946 Mary Burks establishes the Women's Political Council in Montgomery, Alabama.

1949 A bus driver threatens Jo Ann Robinson on a Montgomery bus. The Women's Political Council attempts to improve conditions for African Americans on buses.

1953 African Americans boycott buses for about a week in Baton Rouge, Louisiana.

1955 On December 1, Rosa Parks refuses to give up her bus seat to a white man in Montgomery. Police arrest Parks and take her to jail.

On December 2, African-American leaders agree to support a bus boycott.

On December 5, African Americans conduct a successful bus boycott. The same day, African-American leaders organize the Montgomery Improvement Association (MIA) to lead the boycott. The Reverend Martin Luther King Jr. serves as president of the MIA.

The MIA sets up a car pool by December 13. The car pool transports African Americans during the boycott.

1956 King's home is bombed on January 30. No one is hurt in the attack.

On February 1, attorney Fred D. Gray files the lawsuit *Browder v. Gayle*. This lawsuit challenges the constitutionality of segregation on Montgomery's buses.

On March 22, King is found guilty of breaking a state boycott law. King's lawyers appeal the verdict.

The U.S. Supreme Court announces a decision in the *Browder v. Gayle* case on November 13. The Court decides that segregation is unconstitutional on Montgomery's buses. The bus boycott continues until the Court issues its final order.

On December 20, the Supreme Court releases the order to integrate Montgomery's buses.

The Montgomery bus boycott ends on December 21. King boards an integrated bus that morning.

1957   On January 28, a bomb is discovered on the porch of King's home.

1960   On February 1, four African-American students sit at a lunch counter to protest segregated counters at the Woolworth's store in Greensboro, North Carolina.

1961   The Freedom Rides begin on May 4. The purpose of the rides is to test whether bus stations had been integrated.

1964   On July 2, Congress approves the Civil Rights Act of 1964. This act prohibits segregation in public places.

American Moments

FAST FACTS

The Montgomery Improvement Association (MIA) received about $250,000 in donations. In addition, the organization received letters of support. People from around the world gave money and sent letters to the MIA.

The impact of the bus boycott spread beyond Montgomery. In 1956, African Americans in other Southern cities launched their own bus boycotts. In Alabama, boycotts took place in Birmingham and Mobile. Tallahassee, Florida, also experienced a bus boycott.

In 1962, the MIA prompted the bus company to hire African-American drivers. This victory was the organization's last major achievement. Afterward, it became less active in Montgomery.

The Montgomery bus boycott established Martin Luther King Jr. as one of the greatest civil rights leaders in the United States. On August 28, 1963, King delivered his famous "I have a dream" speech in Washington DC. This speech was one of the most famous moments of the civil rights movement.

Rosa Parks has received numerous awards for her civil rights work. She received the Martin Luther King Jr. Nonviolent Peace Prize in 1980. In 1999, Rosa Parks received the Congressional Gold Medal. This award is the nation's highest civilian honor.

WEB SITES
WWW.ABDOPUB.COM

Would you like to learn more about the Montgomery bus boycott? Please visit **www.abdopub.com** to find up-to-date Web site links about the Montgomery bus boycott and other American moments. These links are routinely monitored and updated to provide the most current information available.

Martin Luther King Jr. delivers his famous "I have a dream" speech in support of the civil rights bill in Washington DC.

GLOSSARY

appeal: to ask a high court to review the decision of a low court.

appellate court: a court that has the authority to review the decisions of other courts.

assassinate: to murder an important person.

bail: money given to authorities in exchange for releasing someone from jail. It is also a guarantee that the released person will appear at his or her trial.

defendant: a person being sued in court.

discrimination: treating a group of people unfairly based on characteristics such as race, class, or gender.

doctrine: a legal principle that has been set down by precedent, or previous rulings.

federal marshals: law enforcement officers who carry out federal court processes. Marshals protect federal judges, attorneys, and jurors. They also respond to situations in which federal law has been broken.

franchise: the right the government gives to individuals or groups to operate a business in a certain area.

indigo: a shrub with leaves that can be used to produce a deep blue dye.

integration: ending segregation. To desegregate, specifically in schools or other public places that were segregated.

labor union: a group formed to help workers receive their rights.

lawsuit: a case brought to court because of a perceived wrong.

minstrel: in the United States, minstrels were white performers who blackened their faces and pretended to be slaves in the mid-1800s. Their impersonations were usually very prejudiced.

plaintiff: a person who introduces a lawsuit in court.

seamstress: a woman who sews clothes.

secede: to break away from a group.

segregation: to put social or political barriers around certain groups of people based on characteristics such as race, class, or gender.

sniper: someone who shoots at people from a hidden location.

unconstitutional: something that goes against the laws of the U.S. Constitution.

American Moments

INDEX